AF306484

GROUPON: THE ONLINE DISCOUNT PHENOMENON

The turbulent history of a record-breaking startup

Written by Charlotte Bouillot
Translated by Rebecca Neal

GROUPON: THE ONLINE VOUCHER GIANT

DISCOUNTS DRIVEN BY THE INTERNET, TRENDS AND SOCIAL NETWORKS

Groupon.com first appeared in 2008, a difficult year for the crisis-hit American economy. The young entrepreneur Andrew Mason noticed that Americans were extremely worried by the decline in their buying power and decided to bring back discount coupons. The site attracts a large number of shoppers by offering huge promotions every day, which are only valid if a minimum number of users sign up for them. This system seems as old as time, but clearly taps into current trends: group buying relies on a network and takes place online; paper coupons become digital; and massive discounts allow customers to treat themselves even during an economic crisis and businesses to attract people back to their shops.

The site's success was astounding: its value reached $1 billion just 17 months after its creation, which is virtually unheard of for startups. After two years, the coupon giant was present in 88 US cities and 22 countries around the world. In late 2010, Mason turned down an offer from Google to purchase the site for $6 billion. When the company went public a year later, it ended its first day with a market value of $16.5 billion.

However, it was not long before cracks began to show: unhappy partners questioned the model's stability, competition increased and huge losses drove away investors. Since 2012, Groupon has fallen off its pedestal, and although the company is reinventing itself, it seems incapable of restoring confidence in its economic model. With the buzz surrounding group buying now a thing of the past, does the coupon giant have a future?

KEY INFORMATION

- **Founders:** Andrew Mason (American musician, born in 1980), Eric Lefkofsky (American entrepreneur, born in 1969) and Brad Keywell (American entrepreneur, born in 1969).

- **Founded:** 15 January 2008 in Delaware, initially under the name ThePoint.com. It officially became Groupon, Inc. on 16 June 2009.
- **Market launch:** November 2008 in Chicago.
- **Sector:** online sales.
- **Key figures:**
  - 2009: net revenue of $30 million.
  - 2010: net revenue of $713 million.
  - 2011: net revenue of $4 billion and 33 million active users worldwide.
  - 2012: net revenue of $5.4 billion and 41 million active users worldwide.
  - 2013: net revenue of $5.8 billion and 44.9 million active users worldwide.
  - 2014: net revenue of $3.2 billion and 53.9 million active users worldwide.
  - 2015: net revenue of $1.47 billion and 48.6 million active users (compared with 260 million subscribers) worldwide as of end of September 2015.

- **Key terms:**
  - **Group buying:** the idea is to get several buyers together in order to increase the sales volume and negotiate a bet-

ter price with the seller. Traditionally practiced by buying professionals or company committees, this buying method has become widespread in the digital era now that buyers from across the world can join forces.

- **Web 2.0:** this expression was coined in 2007 to refer to the evolution of the internet towards greater interactivity with the emergence of social networks, blogs and crowdsourcing, the most notable example of which is the creation of the collaborative encyclopaedia Wikipedia in 2001.

THE EARLY DAYS

AN UNUSUAL PROFILE FOR A FOUNDER

A far cry from the young computer programmers who have founded the majority of startups in the digital era, the man behind Groupon and its record-breaking growth was a 27-year-old musician, Andrew Mason. Mason is a serious music lover: he began playing the piano at the age of six and was in a punk rock band influenced by The Beatles and Cat Stevens while at Northwestern University in Chicago. He was more interested in being part of a counter-culture than in becoming a rock star, and admits that, until the age of at least 25, he was convinced that he would be a professional musician.

Mason's defining quality is his creativity, and he is brimming with ideas. He was born in Mt. Lebanon, Pennsylvania, in 1980 and was 15 when he set up his first company, Bagel Express, to deliver fresh bagels to his neighbours on Saturday mornings.

He taught himself computer programming and secured a job at InnerWorkings, a company founded by the wealthy Chicago entrepreneur Eric Lefkofsky which subcontracts printing work on behalf of its professional clients. He then came up with the idea for a website which would analyse the most popular news topics and summarise the thoughts of the authors of the most widely read articles. The Harris School of Public Policy at the University of Chicago was won over by the idea and awarded him a scholarship in 2006. A few months later, Lefkofsky heard about the idea and offered Mason $1 million to launch the site.

Lefkofsky (born in 1969) is a self-made businessman. He studied law at the University of Michigan, as did his business partner and fellow Groupon cofounder Brad Keywell (born in 1969). The two men used their own money to launch Lightbank, an investment society focused on "disruptive" technologies, in 2010, as well as a number of other companies such as Brandon Apparel (sports clothing) and Starbelly.com (promotional products). Lefkofsky and Keywell are both Adjunct Professors at the University of Chicago, where they teach a course entitled "Building Internet Start-Ups: Risk, Reward, and Failure" together.

DISRUPTIVE INNOVATION

The consultant Benoît Sarazin defines disruptive technologies as innovations which are more effective than existing technologies and which, consequently, supersede them without necessarily creating new markets. An example of this is memory cards, which have partially replaced RAM memories and hard drives.

Mason explained their collaboration to the *Chicago Tribune* in 2010:

> "I never thought of myself as an entrepreneur [...] I have a lot of ideas on things and I like to try and create things. Everything that's happened to me, it's just meeting up with the right group of entrepreneurial people who exposed me to this community and I've learned a ton." (Cited in Markowitz 2013)

AN IDEA OF ITS TIME

When ThePoint.com appeared in 2007, it was a long way from Mason's original idea: it was an online platform to distribute petitions. Initially, it attracted attention because of the outlandish nature of some of its campaigns: for example, thousands of people signed a petition to build a dome over Chicago so that it would stay warm all year round, or to take action against AIDS on the condition that the U2 singer Bono retire from public life. Thanks to this media hype, the young company, which was founded in January 2008, attracted an investment of almost $5 million from New Enterprise Associates in California, the largest venture capital firm in the world.

Although the site ultimately did not generate the traffic it needed to keep going, Mason noticed that one of the most popular campaigns was focused on the need to increase buying power. He then created a blog, getyourgroupon.com, which gave its followers a different promotional offer every day. As there was not much to lose in this new venture, which only needed a small team to find attractive offers every day, the investors encouraged Mason to keep going with it. Offers which reached a minimum number of takers were approved, and every time this happened the site took a commission.

The results were surprising: out of a customer base of 5000 people, the site sold 100 $25 tickets to spend an hour in a sensory deprivation chamber (a soundproof, pitch-dark chamber filled with saltwater at body temperature). In the following six months, Groupon launched its service in Boston, New York and Washington DC, before setting out to conquer Europe by purchasing CityDeal (a similar company founded in Berlin in 2009). Word of mouth attracted huge numbers of visitors and, only 17 months after Groupon was founded, the Russian investment fund Digital Sky Technology, which already had stakes in Facebook (a social network founded in 2004) and Zynga (a social gaming company founded in 2007) injected $135 million into the company, boosting its value to $1.35 billion. At that point, the video sharing website Youtube (founded in 2005) was the only other company to have reached a value of $1 billion so quickly.

SOCIAL SHOPPING

Groupon is a portmanteau which combines the words "group" and "coupon", since the size of the group of customers unlocks the coupon. The principle of group buying is based on the idea of a network, which can be either virtual or real. It has been used for a long time by company committees to obtain advantages for their employees, and brings together a community of buyers who are united by shared interests, forcing them to use word of mouth to gain access to the product or service they want. With the advent of Web 2.0, this can quickly go viral. In Groupon's first six months, over half its users came to the site after hearing about it from their friends.

Like during sales, the buying experience is more important than the product itself: users are part of a lucky few who will get an exclusive offer or find a hidden gem, have to react quickly and wait to see if the offer will get enough takers, and enjoy immediate satisfaction with the confirmation of the deal, even before they get their hands on the final product or service. They can then share this offer with their friends and family and on social networks, which acts as additional marketing for the company. Finally, it is worth noting that most of the offers on the site are for experiences that can be given as a gift or shared with friends (restaurants, trips, flying lessons, spa treatments, and so on).

GROUPON'S EVOLUTION

MASSIVE DISCOUNTS, HUGE SALES VOLUMES

Users who sign up to the site receive a new promotional offer in their city, with a very short expiration date, every day. The discounts offered have to be large enough to generate a significant buzz among a sizeable group of users every day. On top of the discount, sellers have to share the money they make with the site, as Groupon's commission stands at 50% of the price paid by the buyer. This explains why most of the offers come from services (restaurants, beauty, tourism) and the luxury sector, where profits tend to be higher.

Companies using the site benefit from increased visibility, new customers and a sales volume that they would not have been able to reach alone, given that Groupon has several million subscribers and invests heavily in search engine optimisation. According to Mason, two years after the site was created, 35 000 companies had signed up to offer discounts. As a result, Groupon only selects an average of one company in eight, basing this selection on customer evaluations available online, the size of the discount and the originality of the offer compared to those normally offered by the seller. By the end of 2010, 98% of the promotions on the site were approved and Groupon's monthly US revenue stood at $50 million. As of 2011, the company was active in 160 American cities and 35 countries.

A TANGIBLE SERVICE IN THE STARTUP WORLD

The company does not handle logistics itself; rather, it puts customers in touch with local service providers. In this sense, it is a marketing platform, like a city guide or sites that gather consumer opinions, such as TripAdvisor. However, unlike most of the internet companies of its generation, Groupon is a tangible business: in two years, it took on around 4000 employees in some 50 countries, attracted 83 million subscribers worldwide and had a gross revenue of €713 million. Not even eBay, Google or Amazon enjoyed such significant growth so quickly.

Subscribers sign up for a local offer, and then go to a shop to receive the product or service. This represents a tangible business model which attracts a large number of customers, sometimes to very young companies or new services. In this way, the site allows recently founded companies with small or nonexistent marketing budgets to achieve extraordinary sales volumes. For example, in eight hours Groupon sold almost 20 000 tickets for a tour of Chicago's architecture that were reduced from $25 to $12. As we can see, since the beginning the company has relied on its sales force and on a veritable army of writers to come up with enticing offers. These writers were mainly recruited from Chicago's improv scene and are paid a similar wage to journalists.

Did you know?

According to Aaron With, who worked with Mason at ThePoint.com, is active in the Chicago music scene and was Groupon's editor-in-chief until 2014, his writing team wrote the equivalent of a 190-page novel every day during the site's first year!

RECORD-BREAKING RESULTS

The site's growth was meteoric and its sales figures shot up.

Some figures

	2009	2010
Gross revenue	$30 million	$713 million
Net revenue (taking into account amounts paid to advertising partners)	$11 million	$280 million
Number of merchant partners	2900	57 000
Number of subscribers	3.4 million	83 million

The German Samwer brothers (Oliver, Marc and Alexander), who famously made their fortune by emulating successful American concepts such as Airbnb (a platform where individuals can rent out their own homes, founded in 2008) and Pinterest (a social network based on image-sharing, founded in 2010), played a role in the site's growth. When they sold their European clone CityDeal to Groupon, they took over the site's European operations. In just a few months, European sales caught up with and then surpassed American sales. As they only held a 10% share in Groupon, rapid growth before the company's IPO was the only way for the German brothers to ensure quick and sizeable profits for themselves. However, this growth came at a price and, although sales shot up, the company burned through its money far too quickly, mainly due to the number of salespeople needed to forge local partnerships: losses stood at $6.9 million in 2009, before climbing to $450 million in 2010.

AN EASILY IMITATED MODEL

By the end of 2010, 200 sites based on the same model had been launched in the USA and 500 had been launched in the rest of the world, including around 100 in China and 30 in France. Some of them even copied Groupon's domain name and corporate style. All they needed to get started was a team of salespeople on the ground to attract companies and a few good writers to make the offers on the site appear attractive.

Alongside the many short-lived companies, some made a more lasting impact, such as LivingSocial.com, Groupon's main competitor in the USA. This American company was founded in 2007, when Facebook opened up to external developers, and created a number of apps that allowed users to list, note and share many pieces of information on their profile, such as their favourite books and films. The company attracted some 100 million users, bought BuyYourFriendADrink.com and began online marketing activity in partnership with local businesses. At the end of 2010, Amazon, the world leader in e-commerce, invested $175 million in the company, which at that point had high hopes of catching up with Groupon on an international level. However, Mason did not seem worried, as he turned down an offer from Google to buy the company for $6 billion at the same time.

A TURBULENT IPO

Groupon's IPO on 4 November 2011, which was highly anticipated in the new information and communication technologies sector, allowed the company to raise $700 million only three years after its creation, making it the largest IPO for an online company since Google's in 2004. The company's share price increased by 30% on the day of the IPO, before plummeting a few months later, as the majority of analysts had predicted.

Indeed, while the IPO allowed speculators to make a quick profit, few investors seemed prepared to make a longer-term commitment given the company's heavy losses: over $300 million in the first nine months of 2011, in an increasingly competitive sector. A number of web giants had entered the field simultaneously a few months earlier: Facebook with its "Deals" displayed in subscribers' news feeds, the Google Offers system directly connected to Google Maps, @earlybird promotions on Twitter, and the Amazon-backed LivingSocial.

IMPACT

DISSATISFIED PARTNERS

Aggressive promotions and disproportionate sales volumes

Complaints started being made in cities across the world, as sellers criticised the site's operating model. According to them, Groupon's frantic pursuit of aggressive promotions and increased sales volumes caused problems for and even ruined some of its business partners, who could not cope with the excessive number of poorly managed promotions. Restaurant owners in Portland, a Belgian decorator and a patisserie in Reading all complained that they were not able to set their own sales volume, as this was fixed by Groupon and was often unlimited over a given period, and that they were forced to hand over commission fees that were sometimes as high as the full price paid by customers. The result: 8500 buyers for 102 200 cupcakes made at a loss in Rachel Brown's patisserie, and Sylvie Pastur's design boutique forced into bankruptcy.

It seems that the Groupon team was overwhelmed too: the company's marketing director in France, Barbara Weisz, explained in 2011 that the number of unique visitors to the site rose from 3 million to 7 million in the space of just a few months. As a result, deals which previously had 50 takers suddenly had 500 or 1000 people interested. Weisz added that companies generally told Groupon that they wanted to attract as many customers as possible, but in reality neither party was expecting such large orders. However, Groupon was quick to respond, and has now added fixed sales volumes to its contracts. These sales volumes are calculated with business owners directly by a team which is tasked with monitoring partnerships on the ground. A clause focusing on the quality of the deal, which impacts their remuneration in order to prevent abuse or negligence, has also been added.

A difficult customer base

Another pitfall highlighted by companies is the difficulty of creating customer loyalty among Groupon users. Indeed, it seems unlikely that someone who has used a coupon will buy the same product again for four or five times the initial price, when there is almost certainly a similar offer from another establishment available on the site.

Three computer engineers, John Byers and Georgia Zervas from Boston University and Michael Mitzenmacher from Harvard, have tested the model's effectiveness by studying how companies' online reputations change before and after their partnership with Groupon. The results are not encouraging for the companies: although the number of comments on Yelp (a participative reviewing platform) increases considerably when a promotion appears on Groupon, voucher holders typically give scores that are 10% to 20% lower than those given by regular customers (*MIT Technology Review* 2011).

Writers for the food website *Eater* have put forward three main reasons to explain this phenomenon:

- The company was already in trouble and signed a partnership with Groupon in the hope of limiting the damage.

- Voucher users tend to have relatively low incomes and are very demanding with regard to the quality of the offer that has been sold to them. If anything does not meet their expectations, they are prepared to be vocal about it.
- The company was overwhelmed by the sales volumes generated by Groupon and could not maintain a quality service.

Deceptive business practices

In March 2015, a court in Paris ordered the French branch of Groupon to pay a €10 000 fine for deceptive business practices and to pay €1500 in damages and interest to the Union fédérale des consommateurs ("Federal Union of Consumers"), which had embarked on legal proceedings against the site in 2011 because of its inflated and inaccurate discounts. For example, a 47% discount on Brazilian hair straightening was advertised as a 70% reduction on the site, which based the figure on the price for long hair, while a hot stone massage or Thai massage was sold at a 61% discount, whereas the discount on just the Thai message was 55%. The court ruled that, as an intermediary, Groupon was obligated to check whether offers from its partners were correct before publishing them on its site. According to the Direction départementale de la protection des population (DDPP, Population Protection Department in English), which is in charge of fraud prevention in France, some sales-people, who were paid based on the number of contracts they secured, tended to skip certain essential checks and took an overly aggressive approach, sometimes even setting prices which went against the wishes of the service providers (Bergé 2015).

AN UNSTABLE ECONOMIC MODEL

In June 2012, Groupon's share price dropped to below $9, and as a result the company's value plunged below the $6 billion offered by Google in 2010. The company had also been on the Securities and Exchange Commission's radar since its IPO for its allegedly "creative" accounting practices, and in 2011 it finally had to correct its figures. Specifically, its turnover was revised downwards by $14.3 million and its operating losses went up by $30 million.

Groupon was not an isolated case, as the sector as a whole was struggling at that time. For example, LivingSocial laid off over 400 employees in 2012, and needed a cash injection of $110 million from its investors (mainly Amazon, which then held a 31% stake in the company) to get out of its financial difficulties in 2013.

Mason acknowledged that he had built a business based on flash offers that pushed users to buy compulsively, but seemed convinced that Groupon could develop a more reliable business model, in particular through the direct sale of high-tech products (Groupon Goods) and through Groupon Payments, a new, low-cost electronic payments solution which was initially designed for the professionals who managed the daily deals on the site. This new model made the site dependent on offers with a low profit margin: from 2013 onwards, direct purchases with Groupon Goods made up an increasing proportion of purchases on the site. However, these products are much less profitable than vouchers for high added value services (a 20% profit margin for direct purchases, compared with 88% for daily offers).

At the start of 2013, the company announced a net loss of $67.4 million, and Mason was let go in February. In a memo to employees, which he also posted on Twitter, he joked: "After four and a half intense and wonderful years as CEO of Groupon, I've decided that I'd like to spend more time with my family. Just kidding – I was fired today", before accepting responsibility for his dismissal: "If you're wondering why... you haven't been paying attention. [...] [T]he events of the last year and a half speak for themselves." Groupon's share price remained in freefall, closing at $4.53 on 28 February 2013 (Dunan 2013). One year later, LivingSocial's cofounder and CEO Tim O'Shaughnessy announced that he was also stepping down.

DID YOU KNOW?

In summer 2013, Mason released *Hardly Workin'*, a pop rock album inspired by the world of work, with the secrets to succeeding in business featuring heavily in its lyrics.

GROUPON TODAY

2014: a turning point

When Groupon's 2014 financial results were published, its CEO Eric Lefkofsky stated that "2014 was a transformational year for Groupon, as we made significant progress in our strategy to become the world's leading local commerce destination" (*Groupon.com*, 2015).

With over 260 million subscribers, Groupon opted to focus its efforts on customer experience. A new marketplace-style version of the site was launched in September 2014, with the aim of moving away from non-targeted offers that end up feeling like spam and instead encouraging buyers to browse the platform to find the offers that are best suited to them.

ONLINE MARKETPLACES

An increasing number of operators are following Amazon's example and opening their sites up to third-party sellers in order to offer buyers a wider range of products without shouldering the logistical burdens that come with the sale of new products. These "marketplaces" are secure sites that allow buyers and sellers to carry out transactions online, generally with the operator taking a commission on sales.

By emphasising the product, the logo, the location and the proximity to subscribers, the site's similarity to city guides grew more pronounced. These advances were especially necessary given that in 2014 around 50% of Groupon's transactions in France and the USA took place on mobile phones. On 11 June 2014, Groupon launched "Freebies" on iOS. In the USA, it became the number one mobile platform for discount vouchers, sales and promotions, and was downloaded more than 80 million times. By the end of 2014, a total of over 160 million users had signed in to Groupon via either the website or the mobile app.

In order to improve relations with its partners and avoid repeating its past mistakes, the company then began working closely with sellers before their offers went online to come up with an offer that suited their capacities and margins. The company's contracts also became more flexible with regard to discount rates and commissions, which now vary by sector. Following the DDPP investigation, Groupon France also introduced a quality department which was tasked with checking sellers' prices and the accuracy of the offers published on the site.

Future prospects

The company's results from the end of September 2015 confirm that the company is bouncing back in North America, with gross invoiced amounts (the total amounts paid by customers on the platform for their purchases) up 12%, and a reduction in the company's net losses ($27.6 million compared with $73.1 million for all 2014). Subscribers have not abandoned the platform: out of the 260 million people with an account on the site, 53.9 million made a purchase in 2014 (up 23% from 2013), with an average purchase total of $155. Eric Lefkofsky stepped down as head of the company and was replaced by the former Chief Operating Officer Rich Williams, who had three main objectives:

• accelerate   growth   by   attracting   new

customers;
- streamline internal operations and boost efficiency;
- sustainably increase sales of high-margin products.

In line with these aims, the company made plans to invest between $150 and 200 million in a high-impact marketing campaign and to increase its margins, which stand at 46% today compared with 80% in 2011. The streamlining of operations resulted in the company ending its operations in a number of countries starting in November 2016, which led to considerable job losses. Groupon also started working on a food delivery service, Groupon To Go, and began by buying OrderUp, which was present in 40 American cities, in August 2015.

However, investors still did not seem convinced, and share prices fell by 30% following the announcement of the third quarter results for 2015 on 4 November of that year. While the company has proved that it can adapt and seems to be on the lookout for new opportunities, it still does not seem to have found a stable, sustainable economic model almost nine years after it was founded.

SUMMARY

- Groupon was born after a creative young musician crossed paths with two seasoned entrepreneurs. Together, they managed to make discount coupons popular again: with ordinary people's buying power in freefall, vouchers became digital and resulted in a new buying experience which was shared on social networks.

- By combining huge discounts and viral online word of mouth, the company enjoyed global success and record growth. When Groupon went public on 4 November 2011, it closed its first day with a market value of $16.5 billion.

- However, this development came at a price, and the company's burn rate was very high. After the euphoria of its IPO, its value plummeted and losses began piling up, while competition flourished around the world.

- Through its efforts to push up sales volumes, Groupon was accused of drawing businesses into a vicious circle of sales at a loss and dissatisfied customers. Many detractors began criticising the inflated promotions and unequal partnerships, and questioning the company's business model.

- When cofounder Andrew Mason left, the site changed course by developing direct purchases and payment solutions for sellers in its marketplace. Groupon's mobile app was a success and its 2014 figures seemed reassuring. On the back of this success, the company began investing in food delivery in 2015.
- Although the coupon craze seems to be on the wane and the company's business model has yet to stabilise, over the past few years it has demonstrated a remarkable capacity to adapt, and we can be sure that we have not heard the last of it.

We want to hear from you!
Leave a comment on your online library
and share your favourite books on social media!

FURTHER READING

BIBLIOGRAPHY

- Adaken, Y. (2011) Groupon : la face cachée d'une croissance record. *L'Expansion*. [Online]. [Accessed 25 September 2017]. Available from: <http://lexpansion.lexpress.fr/high-tech/groupon-la-face-cachee-d-une-croissance-record_1444553.html>

- Andrieu, O. (2011) Google Offers, concurrent de Groupon, officiellement lancé dans certaines villes américaines. *Abondance*. [Online]. [Accessed 25 September 2017]. Available from: <https://www.abondance.com/actualites/20110426-10843-google-offers-concurrent-de-groupon-officiellement-lance-dans-certaines-villes-ameri-caines.html>

- Auberger, O. (2012) Les bourdes comptables de Groupon tombent mal. *Le Figaro*. [Online]. [Accessed 25 September 2017]. Available from: <http://bourse.lefigaro.fr/indices-actions/actu-conseils/les-bourdes-comptables-de-grou-pon-tombent-mal-173225>

- Bergé, F. (2015) Les faux bons plans de Groupon condamnés par la justice. *BFM.tv*. [Online]. [Accessed 25 September 2017]. Available from: <http://bfmbusiness.bfmtv.com/entreprise/

les-faux-bons-plans-de-groupon-condamnes-par-la-justice-868028.html>

- Brion, R. (2011) Signing Up With Groupon Might Wreck a Business' Yelp Rating. *Eater.* [Online]. [Accessed 25 September 2017]. Available from: <https://www.eater.com/2011/9/12/6654451/signing-up-with-groupon-might-wreck-a-business-yelp-rating>

- Cadoux, M. (2010) Groupon convoité par Yahoo! et Google. *LSA Commerce & Consommation.* [Online]. [Accessed 25 September 2017]. Available from: <https://www.lsa-conso.fr/groupon-convoite-par-yahoo-et-google,117735>

- Corrot, P. (2014) Marketplace : croissance et rentabilité. *Journal du Net.* [Online]. [Accessed 25 September 2017]. Available from: <http://www.journaldunet.com/ebusiness/expert/58492/marketplace---croissance-et-rentabilite.shtml>

- Dion, J. (2010) The Groupon Movement. *Advantage2Retail.* [Online]. [Accessed 25 September 2017]. Available from: <https://a2r.ca/groupon-movement/>

- Dixler Canavan, H. (2015) The Rise, Fall, and Improbable Comeback Strategy of Groupon. *Eater.* [Online]. [Accessed 25 September 2017]. Available from: <https://www.eater.com/2015/8/4/9091069/groupon-to-go-or-derup-delivery-comeback-strategy>

- Dunand, C. (2013) Débarqué, le co-fondateur de

Groupon joue la carte de l'autodérision. *Les Echos*. [Online]. [Accessed 25 September 2017]. Available from: <https://www.lesechos.fr/28/02/2013/lesechos.fr/0202609225860_debarque--le-co-fondateur-de-groupon-joue-la-carte-de-l-auto-derision.htm?texte=groupon>

- Duperron, A. (2013) La cupidité a mené Groupon à sa chute. *L'Express*. [Online]. [Accessed 25 September 2017]. Available from: <https://fr.express.live/2013/3/14/la-cupidite-a-mene-groupon-a-sa-chute-exp-187592/>

- Fauconnier, F. (2010) Amazon investit 175 millions de dollars dans Living Social. *Journal du Net*. [Online]. [Accessed 25 September 2017]. Available from: <http://www.journaldunet.com/ebusiness/commerce/amazon-investit-dans-living-social-1210.shtml>

- Griffith, E. (2015) Counterpoint: Groupon Is Not a Success. *Fortune*. [Online]. [Accessed 25 September 2017]. Available from: <http://fortune.com/2015/03/20/groupon-success/>

- Groupon. (2015) *Groupon Announces Fourth Quarter and Fiscal Year 2014 Result*. [Online]. [Accessed 25 September 2017]. Available from: <http://investor.groupon.com/releasedetail.cfm?releaseid=896215>

- Groupon. (2015) *Groupon Board Names Rich Williams CEO*. [Online]. [Accessed 25 September 2017]. Available from: <http://investor.groupon.

com/releasedetail.cfm?releaseid=940255>

- Hall, J. (2011) Groupon demand almost finishes cupcake-maker. *The Telegraph*. [Online]. [Accessed 25 September 2017]. Available from: <http://www.telegraph.co.uk/finance/newsbysector/retailandconsumer/8904653/Groupon-demand-almost-finishes-cupcake-maker.html>

- Houlihan, P. (2010) Teaching the Secrets of Successful Serial Entrepreneurship. *Chicago Booth News*. [Online]. [Accessed 25 September 2017]. Available from: <https://www.chicagobooth.edu/news/2010-12-07-groupon.aspx>

- Journal du Net. (2010) *Avec @earlybird, Twitter concuerrence Amazon et Groupon*. [Online]. [Accessed 25 September 2017]. Available from: <http://www.journaldunet.com/ebusiness/commerce/twitter-lance-earlybird-0710.shtml>

- Karayan, R. (2011) Groupon : arnaque ou bonne affaire ? *Le Vif*. [Online]. [Accessed 25 September 2017]. Available from: <http://trends.levif.be/economie/high-tech/groupon-arnaque-ou-bonne-affaire/article-normal-201643.html>

- Karayan, R. (2011) Groupon, le site qui croît plus vite que Google. *L'Expansion*. [Online]. [Accessed 25 September 2017]. Available from: <http://lexpansion.lexpress.fr/high-tech/groupon-le-site-qui-croit-plus-vite-que-google_1388001.html>

- Kelleher, K. (2011) The Checkered Past of Groupon's Chairman. *Fortune*. [Online].

[Accessed 7 September 2015]. Available from: <http://fortune.com/2011/06/10/the-checkered-past-of-groupons-chairman/>

- Le Monde. (2015) *Groupon supprime 1 100 emplois et réduit sa présence internationale.* [Online]. [Accessed 25 September 2017]. Available from: <http://www.lemonde.fr/entreprises/article/2015/09/22/groupon-supprime-1-100-emplois-et-reduit-sa-presence-internationale_4767442_1656994.html?xtmc=groupon_supprime_1_100_emplois_et_reduit_sa_presence_internationale&xtcr=1>

- Le Monde. (2011) *Facebook lance un concurrent de Groupon.* [Online]. [Accessed 25 September 2017]. Available from: <http://www.lemonde.fr/technologies/article/2011/04/26/facebook-lance-un-concurrent-de-groupon_1512822_651865.html>

- Les Echos. (2012) *Groupon, LivingSocial : les sites d'achats groupés battent de l'aile.* [Online]. [Accessed 25 September 2017]. Available from: <https://www.lesechos.fr/29/11/2012/lesechos.fr/0202418891471_groupon--livingsocial---les-sites-d-achats-groupes-battent-de-l-aile.htm?texte=groupon>

- L'Express. (2011) *Groupon en Bourse: la fête est finie.* [Online]. [Accessed 25 September 2017]. Available from: <http://lexpansion.lexpress.fr/high-tech/groupon-en-bourse-la-fete-est-finie_1447150.html>

- Mangalidan, J. P. (2013) Groupon: Better Off Without Andrew Mason? *Fortune*. [Online]. [Accessed 7 September 2015]. Available from: <http://fortune.com/2013/04/24/groupon-better-off-without-andrew-mason/>

- Markowitz, E. (2013) The Real Reason Andrew Mason Was Fired. *Inc.* [Online]. [Accessed 25 September 2017]. Available from: <https://www.inc.com/eric-markowitz/the-real-reason-andrew-mason-was-fired.html>

- MIT Technology Review. (2011) *Groupon's Hidden Influence on Reputation.* [Online]. [Accessed 25 September 2017]. Available from: <https://www.technologyreview.com/s/425395/groupons-hidden-influence-on-reputation/>

- Mukherjee, S. (2015) Groupon deals another blow to investors. *Reuters*. [Online]. [Accessed 25 September 2017]. Available from: <http://www.reuters.com/article/groupon-results-research/groupon-deals-another-blow-to-investors-idUSL-3N12Z4FM20151104>

- Muse, H. (2013) Ex-Groupon CEO Andrew Mason Releases Album. *Fortune*. [Online]. [Accessed 7 September 2015]. Available from: <http://fortune.com/2013/07/02/ex-groupon-ceo-andrew-mason-releases-album/>

- Pepitone, J. (2012) Groupon launches credit-cards payments service. *CNN*. [Online]. [Accessed 25 September 2017]. Available from: <http://

money.cnn.com/2012/09/19/technology/grou-pon-payments/index.html?iid=EL>

- Rauline, N. (2014) Pointé du doigt, Groupon déploie une stratégie plus souple. *Les Echos*. [Online]. [Accessed 25 September 2017]. Available from: <https://www.lesechos.fr/02/09/2014/LesEchos/21762-090-ECH_pointe-du-doigt--groupon-deploie-une-strategie-plus-souple.htm?texte=groupon>

- Sarazin, B. (2011) Innovation et rupture techno-logique. *Benoitsazarin.com*. [Online]. [Accessed 25 September 2017]. Available from: <http://benoitsarazin.com/francais/2011/08/innova-tion-de-rupture-et-rupture-technologique.html>

- Steiner, C. (2010) Meet The Fastest Growing Company Ever. *Forbes*. [Online]. [Accessed 25 September 2017]. Available from: <https://www.forbes.com/forbes/2010/0830/entrepre-neurs-groupon-facebook-twitter-next-web-phe-nom.html>

- Yarow, J. (2011) EXCLUSIVE Q&A WITH LIVINGSOCIAL CEO: His Secret Plan For Building The Next Huge eCommerce Company. *Business Insider*. [Online]. [Accessed 25 September 2017]. Available from: <http://www.businessinsider.com/livingsocial-interview-2011-2?IR=T>

- Zetlin, M. (2014) 5 Business Lessons From LivingSocial's Tale of Woe. *Inc*. [Online]. [Accessed 25 September 2017]. Available from: <https://

www.inc.com/minda-zetlin/5-business-lessons-from-livingsocials-tale-of-woe.html>

ADDITIONAL SOURCES

- Groupon's Investor Relations page, featuring reports, results and press releases. <http://investor.groupon.com/index.cfm>

IMPROVE YOUR GENERAL KNOWLEDGE

IN A BLINK OF AN EYE !

www.50minutes.com

Although the editor makes every effort to verify the accuracy of the information published, 50Minutes.com accepts no responsibility for the content of this book.

© 50MINUTES.com, 2016. All rights reserved.

www.50minutes.com

Ebook EAN: 9782808002462

Paperback EAN: 9782808002479

Legal Deposit: D/2017/12603/644

Cover: © Primento

Digital conception by Primento, the digital partner of publishers.